First World War
and Army of Occupation
War Diary
France, Belgium and Germany

19 DIVISION
58 Infantry Brigade,
Brigade Trench Mortar Battery
1 January 1918 - 29 November 1918

WO95/2093/4

The Naval & Military Press Ltd
www.nmarchive.com
Published in association with The National Archives

Published by

The Naval & Military Press Ltd

Unit 10 Ridgewood Industrial Park,

Uckfield, East Sussex,

TN22 5QE England

Tel: +44 (0) 1825 749494

www.naval-military-press.com

www.nmarchive.com

This diary has been reprinted in facsimile from the original. Any imperfections are inevitably reproduced and the quality may fall short of modern type and cartographic standards.

© Crown Copyright
Images reproduced by permission of The National Archives, London, England, 2015.

Contents

Document type	Place/Title	Date From	Date To
Heading	WO95/2093-4		
Heading	19th Division 58th Infy Bde 58th Lt Trench Mortar Bty 1917 Jun-1919 Jan		
War Diary		01/01/1919	30/01/1919
War Diary	NE St Jans Cappel	01/01/1919	31/01/1919
Heading	19th Division 58 Infantry Brigade Brigade Trench Mortar Battery Aug, Sept, Oct, Nov, Dec 1917 Missing		
War Diary		01/01/1918	25/01/1918
War Diary	Line.	08/02/1918	23/02/1918
War Diary		01/03/1918	31/03/1918
Heading	19 Division 58 Infantry Brigade Brigade Trench Mortar Battery. April To Sept 1918 Missing.		
War Diary		01/04/1918	30/04/1918
Heading	To. Brigade Major. 58 Inf. Bde. War Diary For November 1918. O.b.58.L.T.M.B.	30/11/1918	30/11/1918
War Diary		02/11/1918	29/11/1918
Heading	19 Division 58 Infantry Brigade Brigade Trench Mortar Battery. Dec 1918 Missing.		
War Diary			
Heading	6th Wiltshire Vol. 8		

WO 95/2093(4)

19TH DIVISION
58TH INFY BDE

58TH LT TRENCH MORTAR BTY
~~1917 & 1918.~~
1917 JUN — 1919 JAN

WAR DIARY
or
INTELLIGENCE SUMMARY.

58th L.T.M. Bty. Army Form C. 2118.

(Erase heading not required.)

Instructions regarding War Diaries and Intelligence Summaries are contained in F. S. Regs., Part II. and the Staff Manual respectively. Title pages will be prepared in manuscript.

Place	Date	Hour	Summary of Events and Information	Remarks and references to Appendices
	June 1		Battery absorbed into 9/Cheshire Regt. as Infantry - in position near CHAMBREZY.	
	,, 2		Re-organisation of Brigade - Battery attached to 9/Welsh Coy of 58th Bde Composite Batt.	
	,, 3		German attack at 3:10 a.m. - intense barrage, attack beaten off by rifle & machine gun fire	
	,,18th		The 19th Composite Bde relieved by 5th Italian Division	
			marched to CRAMANT.	
	,,20			
	,,21		Moved by bus to BROUSSY-LE-GRAND	
	,,30		at 10 a.m. marched to VASSIMONT.	

WAR DIARY
INTELLIGENCE SUMMARY
(Erase heading not required.)

Army Form C. 2118

JULY 1917.

58th L.T.M. Battery
(July 1st – 31st 1917)

Instructions regarding War Diaries and Intelligence Summaries are contained in F.S. Regs., Part II. and the Staff Manual respectively. Title Pages will be prepared in manuscript.

Place	Date	Hour	Summary of Events and Information	Remarks and references to Appendices
Nr. St Jans Cappel	1st		In camp near St Jans Cappel for rest & training.	
"	2nd		Battery moved to N.16.d.4.6. "The Pits" dug-outs on the York Road. Took over from 57 L.T.M.B. in reserve.	
"	7th		Battery moved to N.16.a.3.5 & occupied dug-outs nr. "Beige Farm". Previous accommodation too small.	
"	12th		Battery Headquarters moved into the "Gurnel Bois" and relieved the 57" L.T.M.Br. Two mortars in position at "Cooksell Post".	
	13th		Two emplacements made in the Front Line (occupied by the Welsh) SW of "Green Wood".	
	15th		These two mortars covered the Junction Buildings. Owing to the activity of Enemy L.M. suspected but on or near SP O.17 d.15.10 , six rounds rapid fire were given at this point. This Enemy L.M. ceased firing.	
	16th		Battery Headquarters advanced from the "Gurnel Bois" to "Tower House" Dug-Out O.14 d.30.45.	
	17th		Two casualties in line near Green Wood.	
	18th		Four mortars in action against the "Junction Buildings" — The Cheshires holding the line. One hundred rounds fired.	
	16th & 17th		Enemy Artillery very active on this part of the line on the occasions of attacks & counter-attacks for the "Junction Buildings".	
	19th		"D" Coy the Welsh relieved "A" Coy of the Cheshires – mortars again active and 35 rounds fired during Enemy Counter Attack.	
	20th		Battery relieved by 56" L.T.M.B. & moved back out of the Line to "Doncaster Huts" Loere, Rest & Training.	
	29th		Proceeded from Loere to N.16.a.3.5, occupying Dug-outs near "Beige Farm" & relieved 56" into reserve.	
	30th		Battery advanced to O.14 d.30.45, occupying "Tower House" dug-out in readiness for the offensive by the 56" Brigade on the morning of 31st.	
	31st		Four mortars were attached to 9" R.W.F.; reserve for the 56" Brigade, & were stationed in Colonel's Yard at the Junction of "Bedon Road". These four mortars were not called upon.	
			Zero hour 3:50 AM for the advance of the 56" Brigade.	

H.C.S. Grant ?/Capt
C 58th L.T.M.R.A.

1875. Wt. W593/826 1,000,000 4/15 J.B.C. & A. A.D.S.S./Forms/C. 2118.

19 DIVISION
58 INFANTRY BRIGADE
BRIGADE TRENCH MORTAR BATTERY
AUG, SEPT, OCT, NOV, DEC 1917
MISSING

WAR DIARY 58-T.M.B.

INTELLIGENCE SUMMARY
(Erase heading not required.)

Army Form C. 2118.

Place	Date	Hour	Summary of Events and Information	Remarks and references to Appendices
			January 1918.	
	1st		The battery was in the line in the Left Brigade sector. four guns were in the line.	
	4/5		The battery was relieved by 142nd T.M.B., moving to Left Subsector Intermediate Line. This was in accordance with 58th Inf. Bgde. O.O. No. 214 dated 3.1.18.	
	5/6		The battery relieved the 57th T.M.B. in the 57th Inf. Brigade Sector in accordance with 58th Brigade O.O. No. 215 of 4.1.18. Seven guns in line.	
	17/18		The battery was relieved by the 56 T.M.B. & moved back into Divisional Reserve in HAWES CAMP, HAVRINCOURT WOOD, in accordance with 58th Inf. Brigade O.O. No. 224, dated 15.1.18. About 80 rounds were fired at enemy posts. T.M. emplacements & M.Gs during this period Jan 5-17. Great difficulty was experienced in maintaining good emplacements owing to adverse weather conditions & the sodden state of the ground after the sudden thaw. However, good results were obtained.	

Army Form C. 2118.

WAR DIARY
or
INTELLIGENCE SUMMARY.

58 T.M.B. Jan (Cont) 1916.

(Erase heading not required.)

Place	Date	Hour	Summary of Events and Information	Remarks and references to Appendices
By our fire.	24/25		The Battery relieved the 57th T.M.B. in the Right Sector in accordance with 58th Inf. Brigade O.O. No 22 & 22446 and 19th Div. G.703. dated 19446. Seven guns were in the line.	
	25-1-16		H.J.Williams 2/Lt For O.C. 58th T.M.B.	

(2)

58th L.T.M. Batty.

WAR DIARY
or
INTELLIGENCE SUMMARY.

Army Form C. 2118.

(Erase heading not required.)

Instructions regarding War Diaries and Intelligence Summaries are contained in F.S. Regs., Part II and the Staff Manual respectively. Title pages will be prepared in manuscript.

Place	Date	Hour	Summary of Events and Information	Remarks and references to Appendices
Line			Ref. "NINE WOOD" 1/10,000. Batty H.Q. L.32.d.08.05.	
			Seven Guns on the line :- R.9.d.85.80, R.4.a.37.15, a.36.17, a.06.13, a.04.63, L.34.c.85.42, C.82.50. } all three	
			Two new alternative emplacements at R.4.c.45.98 & C.45.92.	
			Constructed by the unit during this tour in the trenches.	
			During the tour on the line about 520 rounds were fired (22 days) in retaliation purposes.	
	8/2/18. noon		Hostile posts and machine guns a 40 shoot operation were carried out. Gun at R.9.d.85.80 inspired in new L. Pos at R.10.d.30.75. the target was used for retaliation purposes.	
			Enemy seemed to frequently using 3" Stokes against us but his emplacements could not be located. Surface was then never occupied owing to the fact that all new emplacements were camouflaged causing during which spirits of camouflage	
	9/2/18. 7.30pm		Five rounds were fired on M/G at R.4.d.31.81. the silenced the gun a shorts was observed on the place the next morning.	
	10/2/18. 2.0pm		Enemy Plane engaged by T.M.-3 rounds. Green + 2 rings fused 3 second. Shells had been prepared better results would have been obtained.	
			If a few more shells had been prepared better results would have been obtained.	
	12/2/18		M/G Post at R.4.d.31.81 was silenced with 10 rounds	
	14/2/18		Fifteen rounds fired into R.10.a.80.75 in retaliation for E. T.M. fire	
	15th		Battery relieved by 189th L.T.M.B. 63rd Division.	
	23rd		Battery took over Shelter in TORQUAY from 188th L.T.M.B. 63rd Div.	
			Moved to Camp (PHIPPS) on HAPLINCOURT - BERTINCOURT ROAD	

L.Y. Marshall Lieut
O.C. 58th L.T.M
1-3-1918

WAR DIARY
INTELLIGENCE SUMMARY.
(Erase heading not required.)

Army Form C. 2118.

58th L.T.M.B. March. 1918.

Place	Date	Hour	Summary of Events and Information	Remarks and references to Appendices
	17th		Battery was in training at PHIPPS CAMP (O.6d.4.3, map 57c) on the HAPLINCOURT–BERTINCOURT road.	
	21st	11.30am	Battery moved up to GAIKA COPSE, s.w. of VELU WOOD, with four guns.	
		6 pm	Battery advanced & took up a position on the HERMIES–BEAUMETZ ridge in close support to 57th Inf. Brigade who delivered a counter-attack on DOIGNIES.	
	22nd	6 am	Battery was withdrawn to PHIPPS CAMP.	
		12 noon	The Battery moved to camp 600 yds west of HAPLINCOURT on the HAPLINCOURT–BERTINCOURT road.	
	23rd	1.30 pm	The Battery took up a position with the four guns on the Green Line 50 yds north of the BAPAUME–CAMBRAI road, between FREMICOURT–BEAUMETZ.	
	24th	2.30 pm	Owing to the Brigade on the right having to fall back, the Battery received orders to withdraw. The personnel of the Battery then attached itself to the Inf. owing to its four guns being out of action & other guns & ammunition not being available. A defensive position was taken up 2 Ci yds west of BAPAUME. This position was held for eight hours and at 11.30 pm	

Army Form C. 2118.

WAR DIARY
or
INTELLIGENCE SUMMARY. March. 1918.

Title pages 58. L.T.M.B.

(Erase heading not required.)

Instructions regarding War Diaries and Intelligence Summaries are contained in F. S. Regs., Part II. and the Staff Manual respectively. Title pages will be prepared in manuscript.

Place	Date	Hour	Summary of Events and Information	Remarks and references to Appendices
	25"	12 noon	the position was evacuated, the Inf. retired to a position between GREVILLERS & IRLES.	
		4.30 p.m (night)	IRLES was evacuated & a fresh defensive position was taken up in front of PUISIEUX.	
			The 19 Div. was collected & withdrawn to HEBUTERNE.	
	26"	9 am	The enemy having been repelled on the outskirts of the village we evacuated same & dug in astride the FONCQUEVILLERS-SAILLY road.	
		10.30 p.m	The 4th Australian Div. took over the position & the Battery moved back to BAYENCOURT.	
	27"		Battery not in action.	
	28"	11.30 am	The Battery marched to PAS-en-ARTOIS, arriving at 3 p.m. & was there billeted.	
	29"		Resting.	
	30"	6 am	Battery marched to DOULLENS & entrained at 4 p.m.	
	31st	6.30 am	Detrained at STRAZEELE & en-bussed for billets at LOCREHOF FARM on the DRANOUTRE-LOCRE road, arriving at 8.45 a.m.	

Alfred Williamson
for Capt.
O.C. 58. L.T.M.B.

19 Division
58 Infantry Brigade
Brigade Trench Mortar Battery.
April to ~~Oct~~ Sept 1918 Missing.

58' T.M.B.

WAR DIARY for August, 1918.

INTELLIGENCE SUMMARY.

(Erase heading not required.)

Army Form C. 2118.

56 T M B 4

Instructions regarding War Diaries and Intelligence Summaries are contained in F.S. Regs., Part II and the Staff Manual respectively. Title pages will be prepared in manuscript.

Place	Date	Hour	Summary of Events and Information	Remarks and references to Appendices
	1st		Battery training in FLECHIN sub area.	
	6/7 night of		Battery relieved 76.T.T.M.B. in the HINGES sector. Four guns in the line. Hqrs. established at V30.6.70.65 (36a.S.E.3) B.O.20.254.d/4-5-18.	
	7/8	do.	Two mortars advanced for the purpose of dealing with VERTBOIS FARM, O35d (LES CHOQUAUX) & placed under the command of the O.C. outpost battalion.	
	13"		Two additional mortars placed at outpost of O.C. outpost battalion & situated at W5.6.50.30 (LES CHOQUAUX). From 7-21st the mortars continually harassed the enemy, rear guards, which usually consisted of about ten men a few m.gs.	
	22"		Mortars withdrawn from line & reserve position.	
	23"		Battery took over portion of the 10'L.T.M.B. (4 Div.) Two mortars under the command of O.C. outpost battalion & four mortars covering the crossing of the LA BASSÉ canal in Q.32.c/r Q.33.c, and W3.6. This was in accordance with B.O.20.25p.c.25-5-18.	
	26"		Two additional mortars placed under orders of O.C. outpost battalion.	
	30"		Four of the outpost mortars were moved forward to R.27.d.10.90 & R.27.d.25.50 to cover crossing of the LAWE RIVER in R.28.a.	

H.Y. Hotspall Capt.
O.C. 58 L.T.M.B.

To:-
   Brigade Major,
      55 Inf. Bde.

H/w War Diary for November, 1918

            H.W. Williams
                Lieut.
        O.C. 5&2 T.M.B.

30-11-18
S.M. 295

58' L.T.M.B.

WAR DIARY for November, 1918.
INTELLIGENCE SUMMARY.

Army Form C. 2118.

Place	Date	Hour	Summary of Events and Information	Remarks and references to Appendices
	2-11-18	07:45	The Battery moved by march route from RIEUX to HAUSSY (Ref. 51A. I/40.000) in accordance with 53 Bde Order No. 234 - of 1-11-15.	
	-do-	17:30	Battery marched from HAUSSY to SOMMAING, arriving 19:00 hrs. (Ref. 51A I/40,000).	
	3-11-18	16:15	Battery moved up into assembly positions at L.11 & C.5.3. Hdqrs. were established at MARESCHES (L.25.6.35; ref. 51A/40.20).	
	4-11-18	06:20	The Battery assisted in the attack carried out by 19" Division. One mortar went forward with each of the front two Battalions. On objectives being reached mortars dug up position to cover the valley of the PETIT AUNELLE river. At 16:30 hrs. the two mortars assisted in putting a barrage on ETH in conjunction with an attack on that village by the left Battalion. Adv. Hdqrs. were moved to the CHATEAU at ETH & rear Hdq. were advanced to JENLAIN. (Ref. VALENCIENNES 1:2)	
	5-11-18		The mortars returned throughout the day to refitting task with the moving Battalions. Div. Hdqr. established in ROISIN, a rear Hdqrs. in BRY. (Ref. VALENCIENNES 1:2)	
	6-11-18	13:00	Battery, including staff in BETTRECHIES, guns trained on BOIS D'U.G.I. forward mortars.	
	7-11-18	07:15	Lt. field 20 rounds into BOIS D'U.G.I. in conjunction with artillery barrage.	

58 L.T.M.B.

WAR DIARY
or
INTELLIGENCE SUMMARY.

Army Form C. 2118.

for November, 1918.

(Erase heading not required.)

Place	Date	Hour	Summary of Events and Information	Remarks and references to Appendices
	1/11/18	10.00	The Battery was withdrawn to LA FLAMENGRIE for re-organization.	
	5.11.18	10.00	The Battery moved forward & established itself in the village of BREAUGIES in accordance with 58 Bde. Order No. 256	
(Ref. VALENCIENNES 12)				
	7-11-18		Battery rested.	
	10.11.18		The Battery marched to ETH in accordance with 58 Bde. Order No. 256	
			4/11-18; Hdqrs. were established in the CHATEAU. (Ref. 51 N.W. 1/20,000)	
	11-11-18		Armistice declared – hostilities ceased at 11.00 am.	
	12-11-18 13-11-18		Battery resting & re-fitting.	
	14.11.18	10.20	The Battery marched to BERMERAIN in accordance with 58 Bde. order no. 257	
			2/15-11-18 (Ref. 51A & 51 1/40,000).	
	15-11-18	9P-1	The Battery moved to AVESNES LES ALBERT by march route in accordance with	
			58 Bde. Order No. 258. 2/14-11-18. (Ref. 51A 1/40,000).	
	16-11-18 22-11-18		Light training carried out.	
	23-11-18		The Battery was inspected by J.O.C. B. 17 Division.	
	25-11-18		The Battery marched to CAMBRAI in accordance with 58 Bde. order No. 270.	
	1/26-11-18		(VALENCIENNES 12).	

58' L.T.M.B. —3—

WAR DIARY for November, 1918   Army Form C. 2118.
or
INTELLIGENCE SUMMARY.

(Erase heading not required)

Place	Date	Hour	Summary of Events and Information	Remarks and references to Appendices
	2/11/18	05.45	The Battery entrained at CAMBRAI, moved to the CANDAS area. It detrained at 19.30 hrs in CANAPLES & established itself in billets in that village. (Ref. 58' Pete Order No. 29 x-y 23-11-18) Ref. VALENCIENNES 12 c LENS 4).	

A. Joseph Williams, Lieut
O.C. 58' T.M.B.

19 Division
58 Infantry Brigade
Brigade Trench Mortar Battery.
Dec 1918 Missing

58'L.T.M.B.

WAR DIARY
or
INTELLIGENCE SUMMARY. for January, 1919.

Army Form C. 2118.

(Erase heading not required.)

Place	Date	Hour	Summary of Events and Information	Remarks and references to Appendices
			Throughout the month the Battery was billeted in HALLOY-by-PERNOIS (nr. LENS II) Training in Squad-Arm Drill, P.T. Musketry & the use of the Mortar was carried out. Educational Training in English, Arithmetic & Elem. Maths was also carried out. During the month 14 men were demobilised in accordance with instructions received.	

J M McDougall .... O.C.
58th Light Trench Mortar Battery.

6th Wiltshires
Vol: 8

www.ingramcontent.com/pod-product-compliance
Lightning Source LLC
Chambersburg PA
CBHW081509160426
43193CB00014B/2627